Bond

10 Minute Tests

9-10 years

Sarah Lindsay

English

Nelson Thornes

Test 1: Mixed

Test time: 0 — 5 — 10 minutes

Add the missing commas to these sentences.

1–2 On her way to school, Carys realised she had forgotten her glasses, swimming things, reading book and recorder.

3–4 Dave and Tim struggled through the rain, slipping on rocks and stumbling through the mud, as they hurried to reach cover.

Complete the word sums. Watch out for the spelling changes!

5	depend + able	dependable	8	doubt + ful	doubtful
6	early + er	earlier	9	likely + hood	likelhood *likelihood*
7	cord + less	cordless	10	response + ible	responsible

Give one word for each of these *definitions*. Each word begins with the letter p.

11 A code of letters and numbers at the end of an address to help with the sorting and delivering of mail.

postcode

12 A coin.

pence *penny, pound*

13 A drawing or painting of someone, usually showing their head and shoulders.

portrait

14 A male member of a royal family.

prince

15 The sweet part of a meal.

pudding

Write the following *adjectives* of comparison.

		quieter	*quietest*
e.g.	quiet		
16–17	heavy	heavier	heviest
18–19	good	better	best
20–21	angry	angrier	angriest

Complete each sentence using a different *adverb*.

22 They screamed __loudly__.

23 I swam __quickly__.

24 We giggled __happily__.

25 He whispered __quietly__.

Write the *plural* forms of these words.

26 roof   __rooves__ roofs

27 circle   __circles__

28 lioness __lionesses__

29 quantity __quantities__

30 shelf   __shelves__

Total 24/30

Test 2: Spelling

Write the *contraction* for each of these.

1. have not — haven't
2. could have — could've
3. I will — I'll
4. will not — won't

Write each of these words correctly.

5. thrugh — though ~~through~~
6. medcine — medecine
7. ocurred — occured
8. atmosfere — atmosphere
9. forign — forine
10. extremly — extremely
11. freind — friend
12. carefuly — carefully
13. advertisment — advertisement
14. gratful — grateful

Add the missing double letters to each of these words.

15. a c c idental
16. begi n n ing
17. reco r r end
18. courge r r e
19. a p p earance
20. tomo rr ow

4

Add ary or ery to each of these to make a word.

21 nurs **ery**
22 annivers **ary**
23 scen **ery**
24 burgl **ary**
25 diction **ary**
26 deliv **ery**
27 imagin **ary**
28 ⊘ gloss **ery**

Each of these words has a missing silent letter. Rewrite each word correctly.

29 reath — **breath**
30 ⊘ night — **night**
31 resin — **resign**
32 sene — **scene**
33 ⊘ autum —
34 clim — **climb**
35 ⊘ sord — **scord**

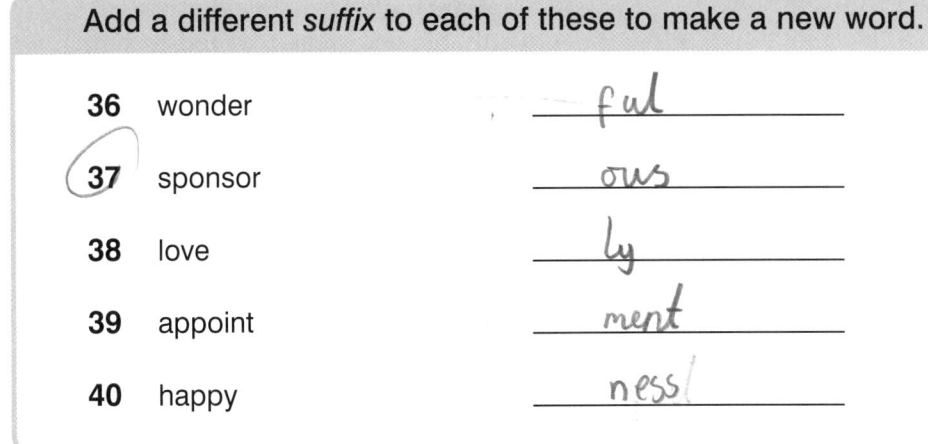

Add a different suffix to each of these to make a new word.

36 wonder — **ful**
37 ⊘ sponsor — **ous**
38 love — **ly**
39 appoint — **ment**
40 happy — **ness**

Total 28/40

TEST 3: Comprehension

Read this extract carefully.

The Very Bloody History of Britain *by John Farman*

The Cunning Celts

[The Celts] came here [Britain] in 650 BC from central Europe apparently looking for tin – please don't ask me why! The Celts were tall, blond and blue-eyed and so got all the best girls right away. This, of course, annoyed the poor Britons even more, but there was not much they could do about it as they only had sticks and fists to fight with. The Celts set up home in the south of England around Surrey and Kent – building flash wooden forts which the poor boneheaded locals could only mill around in awe and envy.

Now England wasn't too bad a place to live for the next few hundred years (providing you were tall, blue-eyed and blond). Then in 55 BC the late Julius Caesar – star of stage and screen – arrived with a couple of legions from Rome, Italy. The refined Romans were repelled, in more ways than one by the crude Celts, who by this time had turned blue (from woad). They did, however, come back a year later with a much bigger, better-equipped army – and guess what – were repelled again.

55 BC – The Romans

You couldn't get away from the fact, however, that the Romans were much sharper than the Celts. They therefore decided that they'd infiltrate peacefully rather than invade; which was just a sneaky Italian trick. How the Celts didn't notice the daftly-dressed Roman soldiers I'll never know.

AD 43 Boadicea

This gradual infiltration took longer than expected and the Romans became rather impatient. Emperor Claudius sent another lot of legions to conquer us properly – which they did – properly! The only real trouble they encountered was a strange woman warrior from somewhere near Norwich. Her name was Boadicea and, from the only available picture I've seen, she seemed to travel everywhere in a very snazzy horse-drawn cart with blades sticking out of the wheels. This must have made parking in London rather tricky, which is probably why she burnt it to the ground. She went on to kill 70,000 Romans but, when they started getting the better of things, poisoned herself.

When In Britain Do As The Romans Do

If you can't beat a Roman, join him. Gradually the hostile Brits came round to the Roman way of thinking. The smart ones even managed to make a few lire and live Hollywood-style, in centrally heated villas covered in naff mosaics. The unsmart ones stayed in their hovels, being only serfs and slaves…. Soon everybody knew their place. Christianity was made the imperial religion and the first two centuries were to be among the most prosperous and peaceful in England's history.

Answers these questions about the extract.

1. Where did the Celts originally come from?
   The Celts came from Central Europe.

2. How did the Britons react when the Celts arrived?
   The Britons was anonnoyed when the Celts arrived.

3. When did the Romans first arrive on British soil?
   The Romans arrived in Briten in 55 BC.

4. Describe one way the Romans were different from the Celts.
   The Romans wore dresses and they were daftly-dressed.

5. Who was Boadicea?
   Boadicea was a worrier and she didn't like the Romans & so she attacked them.

6. Why was Boadicea described in the extract as '**real trouble**' (line 44)?
   Boadica was described as real troble because she wants revenge.

7. What is meant by '**the hostile Brits came round to the Roman way of thinking**' (lines 61–62)?
   It means they want like the Roman way and had things like them.

8. What is the meaning of '**prosperous**' in line 72?
   prosperous means calm.

9. Describe what it was like in Britain during the period of Roman rule.
   Calm and they rather let them settle down instead of fighting.

10. Why do you think John Farman has titled his book 'The Very Bloody History of Britain'?
    He has name his book "The Very Bloody History of Britain" because there is a lot of fighting.

Test 4: **Mixed**

Test time: 0 – 5 – 10 minutes

Add a *verb* to these sentences. Use each verb once.

Eat   Push   Grab   Sit   Watch

1 __Grab__ my coat, it's raining.

2 __Watch__, Tariq is in the next race.

3 __Push__, we have to get the car out the mud!

4 __Sit__ on the carpet, Kate.

5 __Eat__ your breakfast quickly, or you will be late.

Write the masculine gender of these words.

6 daughter   __son__

7 cow   __bull__

8 waitress   __waiter__

9 duck   __drake__

10 Mrs   __Mr__

11 queen   __king__

Underline one *clause* in each of these sentences.

12 The children wanted to walk to school <u>even though it was pouring with rain</u>.

13 Jess worked hard at her story <u>and finished it just before playtime</u>.

14 <u>Although the sun was hidden by the clouds</u> the sunbathers still got burnt.

15 Tom jumped with excitement <u>when he was invited to David's party</u>.

16 The chicken clucked loudly <u>after laying an egg</u>.

8

Write two *antonyms* for each of these words.

17–18 hot   __cold__   __freezing__

19–20 hard   __soft__   __smooth__

21–22 love   __hate__   __hatred__

Match a word with the same letter string but a different pronunciation to each of these words.

quit	dove	watch	cough

23 move   __dove__

24 dough   __cough__

25 suit   __quit__

26 match   __watch__

Write the *root word* for each of these words.

27 homeless   __home__

28 idiotic   __idiot__

29 retell   __tell__

30 mistimed   __timed__

Time for a break! Go to Puzzle Page 42   9   Total

TEST 5: **Vocabulary**

Test time: 0 – 5 – 10 minutes

Write these *abbreviations* in full.

1. TV — Telivision ✗
2. km — Kilometer ✗
3. UK — united kindom ✗
4. approx. — appoxamatly ✗
5. UFO — undentified flying object ✗

Circle the words that can be used for either gender.

6–10

lioness   teacher   farmer

husband   electrician   nurse

(lord)   mistress   uncle

doctor   niece   headmaster

Write two *synonyms* for each word.

11–12	laugh	cuckle	crackle
13–14	shut	close ✓	not opened
15–16	frighten	scare ✓	creep out
17–18	drink	glug	guzzle ✓

10

Write the word for the young of each of these animals.

19 pig   _piglet_ ✓

20 owl   _owlet_ ✓

21 duck   _duckling_ ✓

22 goose   _gander_ ✗

Write a *definition* for each of these words.

23 purchase   _to buy_ ✓

24 supervise   _to watch over_ ✓

25 rehearse   _to do it again_

26 grumpy   _angry, upset_

Mix and match these words to make four *compound words*.

foot   snow   ball   man

27 _football_ ✓

28 _snowball_ ✓

29 _footman_ ✓

30 _snowman_ ✓

Total

TEST 6: Mixed

Test time: 0 — 5 — 10 minutes

Write two *compound words* that begin with the word in bold.

1–2 **play** — playful — playing ?

3–4 **some** — somebody — sometimes

5–6 **eye** — eyeball — eye

Put a tick next to the words spelt correctly and a cross next to those spelt incorrectly.

7   height   ✓
8   weild   ✗
9   relieve ✓
10 beige   ✓
11 retreive ✗
12 greif   ✗

Add the missing punctuation marks.

13 Where are the scissors kept ?

14 Watch out, that car is going to hit you !

15 I will drive you to your piano lesson .

16 Why am I so thirsty ?

12

Write two *onomatopoeic* words that describe the sounds that each of these make.

17–18 volcano   __booming__   __crashing__

19–20 plug hole __gurgling__   __screaming__

Complete the table of *nouns*.

21–28

jealousy   herd   jacket   China
Meena   lifetime   gaggle   hate

Common nouns	Proper nouns	Collective nouns	Abstract nouns
jacket	China	~~heard~~ herd	jealousy
lifetime	Meena	gaggle	haze

Add an *adjectival phrase* to complete each sentence.

29 The __loud, kind, massive__ cockerel, protected his chickens from the fox.

30 The washing dried quickly in the __warm, light__ _____ wind.

13

Total

TEST 7: Grammar

Change the *verbs* in each sentence into more powerful verbs.

1. The dog **ate** its food hungrily. — *gobbled*
2. The children **walked** to the park. — *scurried*
3–4 Mum **said** it was time to **get** out of bed. — *announced* / *clamber*
5–6 As the car **drove** past, it **frightened** the lollipop lady. — *zoomed* / *shocked*

Write two *adjectives* to describe each of these *nouns*.

7–8 a *tearful*, *unhappy* baby
9–10 a *zooming*, *quick* car
11–12 a *colourful*, *pretty* fish
13–14 *blue*, *vivid* sky

Write two examples of each of the following.

15–16 proper noun — *China* — _____
17–18 preposition — _____ — _____
19–20 adverb — _____ — _____
21–22 pronoun — _____ — _____

14

Write four sentences, each with a *preposition* and a *conjunction*.

23–24 _____

25–26 _____

27–28 _____

29–30 _____

TEST 8: Comprehension

Read this extract carefully.

The Ghost of Tantony Pig *by Julia Jarman*

1   A house was being built in Hogsbottom Field, close to Laurie Gell's home.

He strained to see in the darkness. There was definitely an animal in Hogsbottom
5   Field, peering into the trench. Its head was down and large ears covered most of its face, but clearly visible, glistening in the moonlight was the flat edge of a moist snout.

10   For a moment he wondered if he ought to do something about it, tell someone. But then he thought that a pig in a pigfield or an ex-pigfield wasn't exactly an earth shattering event, wasn't a reason to call
15   out the emergency services or even wake his mum and dad…But where had it come from, he wondered. Was it one of Arthur Ram's? Escaped from the new farm perhaps?

20   Now it was making its way along the bar of the H-shape, pausing every now and then to look into the trench and push with its snout.

'Yow!'

25   'No Gingie.'

The pig was deliberate and careful, skirting the other side of the H now, pausing from time to time to examine and push. Stop. Start. Stop. Start. Then left. Left again.
30   Then it was turning round, to come down the other side facing him. Its head swung up and it stood still for a moment, seemed to be looking at Laurie, straight at him, its eyes tawny-gold in the moonlight.

35   'YOW!'

'Gingie. Wait.'

It was walking again. *Walking*. His stomach lurched. He told himself not to be stupid. Of course it was walking. That was what
40   pigs did…And then it was running, not walking now, but rollicking towards the end of the field, where suddenly it vanished.

Vanished. That made it sound like a conjuring trick. Now you see it, now you
45   don't. Had he really seen a pig or was it a cement mixer which looked fat and round?

Who was he kidding? He caught sight of his white knuckles gripping the window sill. The silence was heavy. He felt as if he'd
50   been holding his breath for an impossibly long time. He opened his mouth and the air came out in a gush – and the wind began again, whipping up the soil.

Closing the window he made his way to
55   bed. Mrs Gingerbits pushed under the covers and settled herself in the curl of his stomach. She was comfortable, like a purring hot water-bottle, but he couldn't sleep. Just lay there listening to the wind.
60   Trembling.

…Shouts woke him. It was light. He'd slept late – and there was something wrong at the building site. A ready-mix truck had just drawn up. Laurie dressed and breakfasted
65   quickly, hurried over the road. The driver was still yelling at Charlie Hancock.

'You ordered a ton of concrete, mate, you're getting it!'

And Charlie, very agitated, was pointing at
70   the field. 'Where you gonna put it mate? Look at the so-called footings!'

Laurie was already looking. There was none. The site looked like a badly ploughed field…

Answers these questions about the extract.

1. How was Laurie able to see the pig in the darkness?

   _____

   _____

2. Why was Laurie surprised to see the pig where it was?

   _____

   _____

3. Why didn't Laurie wake his Mum and Dad to tell them?

   _____

   _____

4. What colour were the pig's eyes? _____

5. Copy a sentence in the extract that lets the reader know how Laurie is feeling.

   _____

6. What is 'Gingie'? _____

7. Why in line 49 is the silence described as '**heavy**'?

   _____

   _____

8. Who is Charlie Hancock? _____

9. What is the significance of the final sentence in the extract?

   _____

   _____

10. Describe how you think Laurie is now feeling at the end of the extract.

    _____

    _____

Time for a break! Go to Puzzle Page 43   17   Total

TEST 9: **Mixed**

Test time: 0 — 5 — 10 minutes

Underline the *connectives* in each sentence.

1. Thomas had a friend around for tea but Alex wasn't allowed one.

2. Kay was late for the party despite leaving home on time.

3. Bola lost his race when he tripped over his laces.

4. The dog barked and made the horse rear up.

Write a *definition* for each of these words.

5. opinion _____

6. confide _____

7. truce _____

8. incident _____

9. sudden _____

Rewrite these sentences without the *double negatives*.

10. There wasn't no footballs to play with.

_____

11. They didn't wear no school uniform on the trip.

_____

12. There wasn't no recorder lesson today.

_____

13. The train didn't arrive early at no platform.

_____

18

Underline the correct *verb* form in each sentence.

14   The book (fell/fall) open at the page listing magic spells.

15   When it snowed Raj (sweeps/swept) the drive.

16–17 The groom (was/were) (drove/driven) to the church.

18   Hannah (found/find) her homework just in time to hand it in.

Circle the words which have a soft g.

19–24

geese   magic   legend

   register   wrong

playground   enlarge   dragon

   dungeon   disregard

mirage   ghost

Write whether these sentences are written in the past, present or future *tense*.

25   I am stroking my cat.   _____

26   I will eat my tea.   _____

27   I played football.   _____

28   I made pancakes.   _____

29   I might tidy my room.   _____

30   I am exhausted.   _____

Total

TEST 10: **Sentences**

Test time: 0 — 5 — 10 minutes

Rewrite these sentences, adding the missing punctuation and capital letters.

1–6 did you get my e-mail gareth asked

_____

7–10 nina now she was feeling better had arranged to meet her friends

_____

_____

11–16 would you like some sweets asked deano

_____

_____

Add 'did' or 'done' to each sentence to make it correct.

17 Ivan _____ his homework as soon as he was given it.

18 "I'm sure we have _____ the right thing," confirmed Helen.

19 "_____ you know we had to bring a packed lunch today?" asked Tim.

20 They were sure they had _____ enough to win the competition.

Write these sentences as *reported speech*.

21 "I'm glad you are coming with us, Aunty Sue," said Alex.

_____

_____

22 "We must remember our coats," Mum reminded the children.

_____

_____

20

Add a *phrase* or *clause* to each of these sentences.

23 The rain _____

_____ as they waited under the bus shelter.

24 Najib _____

_____ ran towards the finishing line.

25 The birds _____

_____ as a blanket of snow covered the ground.

26 Michelle slept _____

_____ as they drove up the hotel drive.

Test 11: Mixed

Underline the correct *homophone* in each bracket.

1–2 The (bough/bow) of the boat collided with the (bow/bough) of the tree.

3–4 Aimee's cut on her (heal/heel) didn't take long to (heal/heel).

5–6 The (cellar/seller) sold his goods from the (cellar/seller).

Underline the *pronouns* in the following passage.

7–11

They rushed over the rocks, desperate to get to safety before the waves came in and cut them off from the path ahead. Henry cried as he slipped and hurt his arm. It was wrapped in a jumper, as there was no time for anything else.

Underline one word in each group which is not a *synonym* for the rest.

12	right	decent	honest	untrue	fair
13	quiet	direct	peaceful	calm	tranquil
14	guard	protect	defend	shield	pursue
15	convey	clever	intelligent	smart	brainy
16	offend	question	quiz	ask	interrogate

Rewrite these sentences changing them from *plural* to *singular*.

17–18 The puppies raced towards the balls.

_____

19–23 They ate the ice-creams quickly as they dripped down their arms.

_____

_____

Add a *suffix* to each of these to make new words.

24 end _____

25 help _____

26 colour _____

Write these words in *alphabetical order*.

story   stage   stroll   steak

27 _____

28 _____

29 _____

30 _____

Total

TEST 12: **Spelling**

Test time: 0 — 5 — 10 minutes

Write the *root word* of each of these words.

1   redevelop   _____

2   unanswerable   _____

3   prejudge   _____

4   amusement   _____

5   untidy   _____

6   peaceful   _____

7   electrician   _____

8   interconnect   _____

Add able or ible to each of these to make a word.

9   excit_____   13   flex_____

10 poss_____   14   divis_____

11 inflat_____   15   reli_____

12 resist_____   16   excus_____

Each of these words has an unstressed vowel missing. Rewrite each word.

17 histry   _____

18 avalable   _____

19 lesure   _____

20 vegtable   _____

21 jewellry   _____

22 diffrent   _____

24

Answers

Answers will vary for questions that require children to answer in their own words. Possible answers to most of these questions are given in *italics*.

TEST 1: Mixed

1–2 On her way to school Carys realised she had forgotten her glasses, swimming things, reading book and recorder.
3–4 Dave and Tim struggled through the rain, slipping on rocks and stumbling through the mud, as they hurried to reach cover.
5 dependable
6 earlier
7 cordless
8 doubtful
9 likelihood
10 responsible
11 postcode
12 pound, penny
13 portrait
14 prince
15 pudding
16–17 heavier, heaviest
18–19 better, best
20–21 angrier, angriest
22 loudly
23 gracefully
24 helplessly
25 quietly
26 roofs
27 circles
28 lionesses
29 quantities
30 shelves

TEST 2: Spelling

1 haven't
2 could've
3 I'll
4 won't
5 through
6 medicine
7 occurred
8 atmosphere
9 foreign
10 extremely
11 friend
12 carefully
13 advertisement
14 grateful
15 ac**c**idental
16 begi**nn**ing
17 reco**mm**end
18 courge**tte**
19 a**pp**earance
20 tomo**rr**ow
21 nursery
22 anniversary
23 scenery
24 burglary
25 dictionary
26 delivery
27 imaginary
28 glossary
29 **w**reath
30 **k**night
31 resign
32 s**c**ene
33 autum**n**
34 clim**b**
35 **s**word
36 **w**onderful
37 sponsorship
38 loveable
39 appointment
40 happiness

TEST 3: Comprehension

1 The Celts came from central Europe.
2 *The Britons weren't happy about the arrival of the Celts, though were in awe of their superior skills.*
3 The Romans first arrived in 55 BC.
4 *The Romans were more intelligent / more organised / better equipped than the Celts.*
5 *Boadicea was a female Celt who was a threat to the Romans.*
6 *Boadicea is described as 'real trouble' as she managed to lead a force against the Romans that killed many of the Roman soldiers.*
7 *The unhappy Britains that were invaded by the Romans eventually decided it was better to work with the Romans than against them.*
8 *successful, especially with money*
9 *It was a peaceful period in history when general living conditions improved for many.*
10 *John Farman titled his book as he did, as there appear to have been many 'bloody' battles to win control of Britain through different periods in history.*

TEST 4: Mixed

1 Grab
2 Watch
3 Push
4 Sit
5 Eat
6 son
7 bull
8 waiter
9 drake
10 Mr
11 king
12 The children wanted to walk to school OR even though it was pouring with rain.
13 Jess worked hard at her story OR and finished it just before playtime.
14 Although the sun was hidden by the clouds OR the sunbathers still got burnt.
15 Tom jumped with excitement OR when he was invited to David's party.
16 The chicken clucked loudly OR after laying an egg.
17–18 cold, freezing
19–20 soft, easy
21–22 hate, dislike
23 dove
24 cough
25 quit
26 watch
27 home
28 idiot
29 tell
30 time

TEST 5: Vocabulary

1 television
2 kilometre
3 United Kingdom
4 approximately/approximate
5 unidentified flying object
6–10 teacher, farmer, electrician, nurse, doctor
11–12 *giggle, chuckle*
13–14 *block, close*
15–16 *scare, terrify*
17–18 *guzzle, gulp*
19 piglet
20 owlet
21 duckling
22 gosling
23 *to buy something*
24 *to watch over (a task, activity or person) to make sure everything runs well*
25 *to practise something*
26 *bad-tempered*
27–30 football, snowball, snowman, footman

TEST 6: Mixed

1–2 *playtime, playground*
3–4 *somewhere, someone*
5–6 *eyebrow, eyelash*
7 ✓   10 ✓   13 ?   16 ?
8 ✗   11 ✗   14 !
9 ✓   12 ✗   15 .

Bond 10 Minute Tests 9-10 years: English

17–18 whoosh, crackle
19–20 glug, drip
21–28

Common nouns	Proper nouns
jacket	China
lifetime	Meena
Collective nouns	**Abstract nouns**
herd	jealousy
gaggle	hate

29 brave, fearless and determined
30 strong and warm

Test 7: Grammar

1 gulped, gobbled
2 rushed
3–4 yelled; struggle, jump
5–6 raced; terrified
7–8 beautiful, happy
9–10 bright, shiny
11–12 slippery, silvery
13–14 blue, cloudy
15–16 Wales, Queen Elizabeth
17–18 in, after
19–20 softly, suddenly
21–22 she, they
23–24 I jumped <u>into</u> the swimming pool <u>and</u> made a big splash.
25–26 We sat <u>beneath</u> the tree <u>because</u> the sun was so hot.
27–28 Maddie tried to ride her bike <u>through</u> the gap in the fence <u>but</u> didn't quite fit.
29–30 I put my backpack <u>on</u> my desk <u>then</u> took my seat.

Test 8: Comprehension

1 Laurie was able to see the pig because it glistened in the moonlight.
2 He was surprised to see the pig because the pig was wandering around a building site.
3 Although Laurie realised he was watching something out of the ordinary, he also realised that it wasn't so important that he needed to wake his parents.
4 tawny-gold
5 'His stomach lurched'; 'He caught sight of his white knuckles gripping the window-sill'.
6 Laurie's cat Mrs Gingerbits.
7 The silence is described as 'heavy' because it is an uncomfortable silence, loaded with worry and concern for Laurie.
8 the builder
9 It proved that Laurie had seen a pig because the land was destroyed by the pig's rooting around.
10 Your child's description of how Laurie might now be feeling, e.g. frightened, worried, shocked.

Test 9: Mixed

1 Thomas had a friend around for tea <u>but</u> Alex wasn't allowed one.
2 Kay was late for the party <u>despite</u> leaving home on time.
3 Bola lost his race <u>when</u> he tripped over his laces.
4 The dog barked <u>and</u> made the horse rear up.
5 a statement of ideas or beliefs
6 to trust someone with a secret
7 an agreement between two parties to stop fighting for a certain length of time
8 an event or happening
9 happening quickly or unexpectedly
10 There were no footballs to play with / There weren't any footballs to play with.
11 They didn't wear school uniform on the trip.
12 There wasn't a recorder lesson today. / There was no recorder lesson today.
13 The train didn't arrive early at the platform.
14 fell   **15** swept
16–17 was; driven
18 found

19–24 magic, legend, register, enlarge, dungeon, mirage
25 present   **28** past
26 future   **29** future
27 past   **30** present

Test 10: Sentences

1–6 "Did you get my e-mail?" Gareth asked.
7–10 Nina, now she was feeling better, had arranged to meet her friends.
11–16 "Would you like some sweets?" asked Deano.
17 did   **19** Did
18 done   **20** done
21 Alex said he was glad Aunty Sue was coming with them.
22 Mum reminded the children not to forget/to remember their coats.
23–26 Children's own answers such as, Najib, who was the fastest runner in the class, ran towards the finishing line.

Test 11: Mixed

1–2 bow bough
3–4 heel heal
5–6 seller cellar
7–11 <u>They</u> rushed over the rocks, desperate to get to safety before the waves came in and cut <u>them</u> off from the path ahead. Henry cried as <u>he</u> slipped and hurt his arm. <u>It</u> was wrapped in a jumper, as there was no time for <u>anything</u> else.
12 untrue   **15** convey
13 direct   **16** offend
14 pursue
17–18 The puppy raced towards the ball.
19–23 S/he ate the ice-cream quickly as it dripped down his/her arm.
24 endless, ending
25 helpful, helper, helping
26 colourless, colourful

A2

Bond 10 Minute Tests 9-10 years: English

27 stage	29 story
28 steak	30 stroll

Test 12: Spelling

1 develop	21 jewellery
2 answer	22 different
3 judge	23 They're
4 amuse	24 there
5 tidy	25 their
6 peace	26 There
7 electric	27–28 They're
8 connect	their
9 excitable	29 veil
10 possible	30 height
11 inflatable	31 foreign
12 resistible	32 cashier
13 flexible	33 relief
14 divisible	34 receipt
15 reliable	35 flatter
16 excusable	36 hoping
17 history	37 busier
18 available	38 amused
19 leisure	39 entering
20 vegetable	40 relieved

Test 13: Comprehension

1 We don't know. It was written anonymously.
2 They sang.
3 *She wanted to wear something more practical outside.*
4 white
5 caught sight of
6 *She wanted a freer, or more exciting life.*
7 *The lord felt upset and surprised. He wanted to try to persuade her to come back home.*
8 messy, dirty, unclean, untidy
9 *the language it is written in, the description of the servants, horse, home etc.*
10 *happy, relieved and free to have left the home where she obviously felt unhappy*

Test 14: Mixed

1 pizza – Italy
2 boomerang – Australia
3 restaurant – France
4 pyjamas – India
5 adverb
6 verb
7 preposition
8 abstract noun/noun/verb
9 pronoun
10 adjective/verb
11 *Chloe asked if they could go swimming.*
12 *The Bayliss family complained that they always have fish fingers for tea.*
13 *Dad suggested they drive past Buckingham Palace.*
14 *Elizabeth laughed, saying she loved pony riding.*
15 misquote   18 prearrange
16 misfortune 19 misspell
17 premature
20–30 "I feel so tired," complained Jim.
"That's because it is one o'clock in the morning!" said the babysitter.

Test 15: Vocabulary

1 impossiblility   6 smart
2 irritable   7 smirk
3 island   8 smoke
4 ivy   9 smother
5 investigate   10 smuggle
11–14 *computer, compact disc, ipod, mobile phone, television*
15 heehaw   17 honk
16 roar   18 cluck
19–20 *untidy, messy*
21–22 *sad, unhappy*
23–24 *weak, feeble*
25–26 *damp, wet*
27 cloud   29 fence
28 cats   30 music

Test 16: Mixed

1 HRH   3 Dec
2 DIY   4 PM

5 OAP   9–10 to, to
6 PO   11 two
7 too   12 to
8 Too
13–16 "Time for your piano lesson," Mum called. (or!)
17–20 "Where have you put my phone?" asked Rebecca.
21 *sparkly, glamourous*
22 *terrified, prickly*
23 *mad, strict*
24 *empty, bustling*
25 *The rain poured but they still had a BBQ.*
26 *There was a fire in the school hall although it didn't do much damage.*
27 *Jake threw the ball and it landed in someone's garden.*
28 disrespect   30 whisper
29 daft

Test 17: Grammar

1–8

Common nouns	Proper nouns
insects	Jake
pets	Tyrone
Collective nouns	**Abstract nouns**
swarms	dislike
colonies	fear

9 *the old and musty book*
10 *the long, hot and busy summer*
11 *the fearless and amazing acrobat*
12 *the beautiful and interesting country of India*
13 *a lovely, old family photograph*
14 because
15 although
16 but
17 as
18 so
19–20 *Everyone watched (anxiously) as the rope was lowered over the edge of the cliff.*
21–22 *The children wandered off (gloomily) despite being given some money to spend.*

A3

Bond 10 Minute Tests 9–10 years: English

23–24 Nazar worked (happily) knowing as soon as he'd finished cleaning the car he could go <u>inside</u> to watch the rugby match.

25–30 Three sentences, each sentence containing two possessive pronouns, e.g. <u>Ours</u> is bigger than <u>theirs</u>.

11 suffixes
12 under
13 at
14 with
15 above
16 on
17 adder
18 alligator
19 ant
20 antelope
21 You'll
22 mustn't
23 Let's
24 could've
25 I'd
26 though
27 weight
28 grown
29 hour
30 door

Test 18: Comprehension

1 Nairobi
2 (1) dirt instead of paved roads (2) background noise of cockerels and cows instead of car horns and radios
3 the daughter of Boniface and Pauline Kamaus
4 one's native language/ the language a person first learns to speak
5 Many of the plants grown in Murang'a differ to those grown here because of the different climate.
6 Pauline felt comfortable back home with her parents and possibly liked getting away from the busy city.
7–8 Joyce and Sharon's grandparents must get their water from a stream and grow their own food. Most grandparents in England get their water from taps in their house and buy food in shops.
9 If they moved back to the country, getting a job to earn enough money to take care of the young family would be much harder than it is in the city.
10 the watching of TV, enjoying time with cousins, staying with grandparents etc.

Test 19: Mixed

1 section
2 unoccupied, empty
3 selfish
4 obvious
5 recall
6 torches
7 princesses
8 thieves
9 bikes
10 valleys

Test 20: Sentences

1–4 Two sentences, each with two correctly marked commas, e.g. Katy put her pencil, pen, ruler and sharpener in her backpack.
5 It is time to meet in the park.
6 We are going on holiday to Devon.
7 Liverpool won the Premiership.
8 The school is closed because of the snow that fell last night.
9 The cows are milked twice a day.
10 are **12** is **14** Is
11 are **13** is **15** are
16–28 "What time does the film start?" asked Brenna. She was worried they wouldn't have time to buy popcorn before it started. "We have plenty of time," her dad reassured her.

Puzzle 1

sausage – usage, age, sage, us, sag, a
wardrobe – ward, robe, rob, war, be, a
mathematics – math, at, the, he, them, mat, hem, tic, tics, thematic, thematics, a
scarecrow – scar, scare, car, row, are, crow, care, a
coincidentally – coincide, coincidental, dent, dental, tall, den, ally, all, incident, incidental, incidentally, tally, in, coin, a

Puzzle 2

An adjective beginning with each letter of the alphabet – 'x' will be the biggest challenge and a dictionary could be used to help with this one!

Puzzle 3

Your child's own answers to a number of word problems e.g.
marmalade maroon marry mask mass master match material maths matter mattress maximum mayor meadow mean measles **measure**
A word with all vowels = aeronautics

Puzzle 4

north = thorn
parties = pirates
vowels = wolves
team = meat, mate, tame
eighth = height
thicken = kitchen
Three anagrams chosen by your child

Puzzle 5

silly – sensible
official – unofficial
dissatisfied – happy
huge – tiny
incorrect – right
unclear – legible
smooth – rough

A4

Write there, their or they're in each gap.

23 _____ going to be late.

24 We must be nearly _____ by now!

25 We'll collect _____ sleeping bags on the way home.

26 _____ seems to be a problem with that car.

27–28 _____ great friends but they argue about _____ favourite football teams all the time!

Add ie or ei to each of these to make a word.

29 v_ _l

30 h_ _ght

31 for_ _gn

32 cash_ _r

33 rel_ _f

34 rec_ _pt

Complete these word sums. Watch out for the spelling changes!

35 flat + er = _____

36 hope + ing = _____

37 busy + er = _____

38 amuse + ed = _____

39 enter + ing = _____

40 relief + ed = _____

Time for a break! Go to Puzzle Page 44

Test 13: Comprehension

Read this poem carefully.

The Wraggle Taggle Gypsies

1 There were three gypsies a-come to my door,
And down-stairs ran this lady, O!
One sang high, and another sang low,
5 And the other sang, Bonny, bonny, Biscay, O!

Then she pulled off her silk finished gown
And put on hose of leather, O!
10 The ragged, ragged rags about our door –
She's gone with the wraggle taggle gypsies, O!

It was late last night, when my lord came home,
15 Enquiring for his a-lady, O!
The servants said on every hand:
'She's gone with the wraggle taggle gypsies, O!'

'O saddle to me my milk-white steed,
20 Go and fetch me my pony, O!
That I may ride and seek my bride,
Who is gone with the wraggle taggle gypsies, O!'

O he rode high and he rode low,
25 He rode through woods and copses too,
Until he came to an open field,
And there he espied his a-lady, O!

'What makes you leave your house and land?
30 What makes you leave your money, O!
What makes you leave your new-wedded lord;
To go with the wraggle taggle gypsies, O!'

35 'What care I for my house and my land?
What care I for my money, O?
What care I for my new-wedded lord?
I'm off with the wraggle taggle gypsies, O!'

40 'Last night you slept on a goose-feather bed,
With the sheet turned down so bravely, O!
And to-night you'll sleep in a cold open
45 field,
Along with the wraggle taggle gypsies, O!'

'What care I for a goose-feather bed,
With the sheet turned down so bravely,
50 O!
For to-night I shall sleep in a cold open field,
Along with the wraggle taggle gypsies, O!'

Anon.

Answer these questions about the poem.

1 Who wrote this poem? _____

2 What did the gypsies do at the lady's door?
   _____

3 Why do you think the lady took off her silk gown?
   _____

4 What colour was the lord's horse?
   _____

5 What does the word '**espied**' (line 27) mean?
   _____

6 Why did the lady leave with the gypsies?
   _____
   _____

7 Describe how the lord felt about his wife leaving.
   _____
   _____

8 What impression does the phrase '**wraggle, taggle**' give you about the gypsies?
   _____

9 How do we know this poem was not written in the present day?
   _____

10 At the end of the poem, how do you think the lady is feeling? Why?
    _____
    _____

TEST 14: **Mixed**

Test time: 0 — 5 — 10 minutes

Draw lines to link each word with the country from which it is borrowed.

1 pizza   Australia

2 boomerang   India

3 restaurant   Italy

4 pyjamas   France

Which part of speech is each of these words?

5   beautifully   _____

6   wrote   _____

7   behind   _____

8   love   _____

9   they   _____

10 blunt   _____

Change these sentences into *reported speech*.

11 "Can we go swimming?" Chloe asked.
    _____

12 "We always have fish fingers for tea," complained the Bayliss family.
    _____

13 "Let's drive past Buckingham Palace," suggested Dad.
    _____

14 "I love pony riding!" laughed Elizabeth.
    _____

Select the *prefix* mis or pre for each of these words.

15 _____ quote

16 _____ fortune

17 _____ mature

18 _____ arrange

19 _____ spell

Rewrite the following correctly.

20–30 i feel so tired complained jim that's because it is one o'clock in the morning said the babysitter

_____

_____

_____

_____

_____

TEST 15: Vocabulary

Write one word for each *definition*. Each word begins with the letter i.

1. Something that cannot be done under any circumstances. _____
2. Grumpy and easily annoyed. _____
3. A piece of land surrounded by water. _____
4. A leafy, evergreen plant that can climb up walls. _____
5. To look into something or someone. _____

Write these words in *alphabetical order*.

smirk   smother   smart   smuggle   smoke

6. _____
7. _____
8. _____
9. _____
10. _____

Write four words that have been invented in the last 100 years.

11. _____
12. _____
13. _____
14. _____

Write an *onomatopoeic* word for the sound that each of these animals makes.

15 donkey _____

16 lion _____

17 goose _____

18 hen _____

Write two *antonyms* for each of these words.

19–20 tidy _____ _____

21–22 happy _____ _____

23–24 strong _____ _____

25–26 dry _____ _____

Choose a word to complete each expression.

fence   cloud   music   cats

27 Every _____ has a silver lining.

28 It is raining _____ and dogs.

29 To sit on the _____.

30 To face the _____.

Test 16: Mixed

Write the *abbreviations* of these words.

1. His Royal Highness _____
2. do it yourself _____
3. December _____
4. Prime Minister _____
5. old age pensioner _____
6. Post Office _____

Add 'to', 'too' or 'two' to each sentence to make it correct.

7. The chips were _____ hot.
8. _____ many people were trying to get on the bus.
9–10. Danielle wanted _____ go _____ Rupa's party.
11. The _____ boys ran as fast as they could.
12. The teacher spoke sternly _____ the giggling children.

Rewrite these sentences with the missing punctuation.

13–16. Time for your piano lesson Mum called

_____

_____

17–20. Where have you put my phone asked Rebecca

_____

_____

32

Add an interesting *adjective* to describe each of these *nouns*.

21   the _____ dress

22   the _____ hedgehog

23   the _____ professor

24   the _____ restaurant

Use *connectives* to write each of these pairs of short sentences as one sentence.

25   The rain poured. They still had a BBQ.

_____

26   There was a fire in the school hall. It didn't do much damage.

_____

_____

27   Jake threw the ball. It landed in someone's garden.

_____

Write an *antonym* for each of these words.

28   respect   _____

29   clever   _____

30   scream   _____

Time for a break! Go to Puzzle Page 45

TEST 17: Grammar

Complete the table using some of the *nouns* in the short passage.

1–8 Jake had a dislike of insects. He worried that swarms or colonies might attack him! Tyrone wanted to help him get over his fear and so told him to think of them as pets!

Common nouns	Proper nouns	Collective nouns	Abstract nouns

Write an *adjectival phrase* about each of these *nouns*.

9   a book

10   the summer

11   an acrobat

12   India

13   a photograph

Complete each sentence by adding a different *conjunction*.

14   Faye couldn't go to the party _____ she was unwell.

15   The flowers opened in the sun _____ there was a cold wind blowing.

16   Annie was painting in the kitchen _____ the cat had taken cover under the table!

17   Gareth was terrified _____ the spider made its way towards him.

18   They missed their train _____ they had to catch a bus.

Circle the *adverbs* and underline the *prepositions* in these sentences.

19–20 Everyone watched anxiously as the rope was lowered over the edge of the cliff.

21–22 The children wandered off gloomily despite being given some money to spend.

23–24 Nazar worked happily knowing as soon as he'd finished cleaning the car he could go inside to watch the rugby match.

Write three sentences, each including two *possessive pronouns*.

25–26 _____

_____

27–28 _____

_____

29–30 _____

_____

35 Total

Test 18: Comprehension

Read this article carefully.

The Kamaus from Kenya *by Xan Rice*

For the half-term holidays, the Kamaus went upcountry to the farming village where Pauline's parents live. Though just 60 miles from the Kenyan capital, Nairobi, Murang'a is a very different world.

Tarred road gives way to dirt; concrete urban sprawl to rich red soil. The background noise comes from cockerels and cows rather than the car hooters and blaring radios of the big city.

The children love visiting their grandparents. Though Joyce is something of a TV addict, she and Sharon revel in the wide-open space and the chance to play all day with their cousins, who seldom make it to Nairobi.

They also practise speaking Kikuyu, which should be their mother tongue. Boniface and Pauline are native Kikuyu speakers, but at home in Nairobi they communicate in Kiswahili, which together with English is Kenya's official national language and predominates in the urban areas. At school, Joyce learns only the two national languages, and her Kikuyu is rusty at best....

Pauline also enjoys being home with her parents. As their first-born child, she assumes the greatest responsibility of all her siblings for her parents' well-being. For now they are doing just fine.

On a hectare of land, they grow maize, beans, bananas, sugarcane, sweet potatoes, avocados and coffee. They also have a cow, a few goats, chickens and rabbits. Some of the produce is eaten; the rest taken to the wholesale market.

Pauline quickly slipped back into the lifestyle of her youth. She fetched water from the nearby stream. She worked in the fields. In the evenings, she helped prepare dinner. It made her nostalgic, and after the holiday Pauline told Boniface that they should think of moving to the countryside.

But Boniface was not tempted. Murang'a in particular, just a few miles from where he was raised, holds too many memories of a difficult childhood. Then there is the issue of work. Being a taxi-driver in Nairobi is a tough job, but at least it provides a steady income – far more than he could ever make as a small-scale farmer.

Saturday Guardian 7th July 2007

Copyright © Guardian News & Media Ltd 2007

Answer these questions about the article.

1. Where do the Kamaus live in Kenya?

2. List two differences between life in Murang'a and life in Nairobi.

3. Who is Joyce?

4. What is a '**mother tongue**' (line 19)?

5. What do you notice about the foods grown in Murang'a compared to in England?

6. Why do you think Pauline wanted to move back to the countryside?

7–8. Describe two ways the life of these children's grandparents differs from the lives of the grandparents of many children in the United Kingdom.

9. What is meant by the sentence '**Then there is the issue of work**' (lines 51–52)?

10. How many similarities can you list between your family and the Kamaus family?

TEST 19: **Mixed**

Test time: 0 — 5 — 10 minutes

Write a *synonym* for each of the words in bold.

1 Please pass me the **part** of the newspaper that is for children.

  _____

2 The bungalow in our street has been **vacant** for a year. _____

3 She is so **stingy**, she never shares her colouring pens. _____

4 It was **clear** from his pale face that he had hurt his ankle badly.

  _____

5 Gemma, can you **remember** what I asked you to do next?

  _____

Write the *plural* forms of these words.

6 torch _____ 9 bike _____

7 princess _____ 10 valley _____

8 thief _____ 11 suffix _____

Circle the *preposition* in each of these sentences.

12 George's shoes were hidden under the sofa.

13 Tea will be ready at six-thirty.

14 Helen mended her broken tyre with a puncture repair kit.

15 The river flooded above the height of the fence posts.

16 The dog slept soundly on his owner's bed!

Put these animals in *alphabetical order*.

antelope   adder   alligator   ant

17 (1) _____

18 (2) _____

19 (3) _____

20 (4) _____

Add the missing apostrophes.

21 Youll have to learn your spellings for the test!

22 We mustnt be late.

23 Lets buy some sweets, please.

24 You couldve stayed longer.

25 I wish Id brought my bike to ride.

Write a word with the same letter string as underlined in each of these words, but a different pronunciation.

26 t<u>ough</u>   _____

27 h<u>eigh</u>t   _____

28 br<u>ow</u>n   _____

29 f<u>our</u>   _____

30 sp<u>oo</u>n   _____

39

Total

TEST 20: **Sentences**

Test time: 0 — 5 — 10 minutes

Write two sentences. Each sentence needs to have two commas.

1–2

_____

_____

3–4

_____

_____

Write these questions as statements.

5   Is it time to meet in the park?

_____

6   Are we going on holiday to Devon?

_____

7   Did Liverpool win the Premiership?

_____

8   Is the school closed because of the snow that fell last night?

_____

9   Are the cows milked twice a day?

_____

40

Add 'is' or 'are' to each sentence to make it correct.

10 On Saturday, Kellie and Sarah _____ coming for a sleepover.

11 We _____ still waiting for the train!

12 Hussan _____ working hard to improve his skateboarding.

13 Daniel _____ going to walk the dog when he gets home.

14 _____ Sam's answer right?

15 Where _____ your gloves?

Rewrite this short passage correctly.

16–28

what time does the film start asked brenna

she was worried they wouldn't have time to buy popcorn before it started

we have plenty of time her dad reassured her

_____

_____

_____

_____

_____

_____

_____

_____

Time for a break! Go to Puzzle Page 46

Puzzle 1

Each of these words has within it a number of smaller words.
How many smaller words can you find in each word, without rearranging the letters or missing letters out?

sausage

_____

wardrobe

_____

mathematics

_____

scarecrow

_____

coincidentally

_____

Find your own word that has at least five smaller words within it.
Try it out on someone.

_____

Puzzle 2

Can you find 26 different *adjectives*, each beginning with a different letter of the alphabet?

a _____   b _____   c _____

d _____   e _____   f _____

g _____   h _____   i _____

j _____   k _____   l _____

m _____   n _____   o _____

p _____   q _____   r _____

s _____   t _____   u _____

v _____   w _____   x _____

y _____   z _____

Circle the five most imaginative *adjectives* you have written.

Puzzle 3

Answer these problems, then try again using a dictionary!

List as many words as you can that lie alphabetically between the words 'marmalade' and 'measure'.

My unaided answers

My answers with the help of a dictionary

Write the longest word you can think of.

_____

Write the longest word you can find in a dictionary.

_____

Write a word with as many vowels as possible.

_____

Write a word from the dictionary that uses as many vowels as possible.

_____

Can you find a word in the dictionary that uses all of the vowel letters?

_____

Puzzle 4

Look carefully at these words.

spoon   **sister**   **petal**

If the letters in each word are rearranged they will make a new word. These words are called anagrams.

spoon	=	**snoop**
sister	=	**resist**
petal	=	**plate**

Your challenge is to find the hidden words by rearranging the letters in these words, as quickly as possible!

north   _____

parties   _____

vowels   _____

team   _____

eighth   _____

thicken   _____

Now make three anagrams of your own.

_____ = _____

_____ = _____

_____ = _____

Puzzle 5

g	f	r	a	t	u	h	m	c	i
s	e	n	s	i	b	l	e	t	p
d	w	e	m	n	s	q	h	o	p
v	h	q	c	y	n	g	c	r	e
t	e	a	k	d	i	y	a	o	g
i	e	j	p	r	k	r	d	u	i
t	w	g	j	p	o	d	s	g	b
e	l	s	i	a	y	n	e	h	y
u	n	o	f	f	i	c	i	a	l
p	i	t	l	e	g	i	b	l	e

Look in the wordsearch to find *antonyms* for the following words.
Write the words you have found.

silly   _____

official   _____

dissatisfied   _____

huge   _____

incorrect   _____

unclear   _____

smooth   _____

Key words

Some special words are used in this book. You will find them picked out in *italics*. These words are explained here.

abbreviation	a word that has been shortened
abstract noun	a noun referring to a concept or idea, e.g. love, beauty
adjectival phrase	a group of words describing a noun
adjective	a word that describes somebody or something
adverb	a word that gives extra meaning to a verb
alphabetical order	words arranged in the order of the letters in the alphabet
antonym	a word with a meaning opposite to another word, e.g. hot/cold
clause	a section of a sentence with a verb
collective noun	a word referring to a group or collection of things, e.g. a swarm of bees
common noun	a general name of a person, place or thing, e.g. boy, office
compound word	a word made up of two other words, e.g. football
conjunction	a word used to link sentences, phrases or words, e.g. and, but
connective	a word or words that join clauses or sentences
contraction	two words shortened into one with an apostrophe placed where the letter/s have been dropped, e.g. do not/don't
definition	the meaning of a word
double negative	two negative words in a sentence that make the idea in the sentence positive, e.g. *I am not going to buy no bike* (which means I am going to buy a bike)
homophone	a word that has the same sound as another but a different meaning or spelling, e.g. right/write
noun	a naming word
onomatopoeic	a word that echoes a sound, associated with its meaning, e.g. hiss
phrase	a group of words that do not contain both a subject and a verb
plural	more than one, e.g. cats
possessive pronoun	a pronoun showing to whom something belongs, e.g. mine, ours
prefix	a group of letters added to the beginning of a word, e.g. un, dis
preposition	a word that links nouns and pronouns to other parts of a sentence, e.g. he sat *behind* the door
pronoun	a word that can be used instead of a noun
proper noun	the specific name or title of a person or a place, e.g. Ben, London
reported speech	what has been said without using the exact words or speech marks
root word	a word to which a prefix or suffix can be added to make another word, e.g. quick – *quickly*
singular	one of something, e.g. cat
suffix	a group of letters added to the end of a word, e.g. ly, ful
synonym	a word with a very similar meaning to another word, e.g. quick/fast
tense	tells when an action was done, e.g. past (*I slept*), present (*I am sleeping*) or future (*I will sleep*)
verb	a 'doing' or 'being' word

Progress Grid

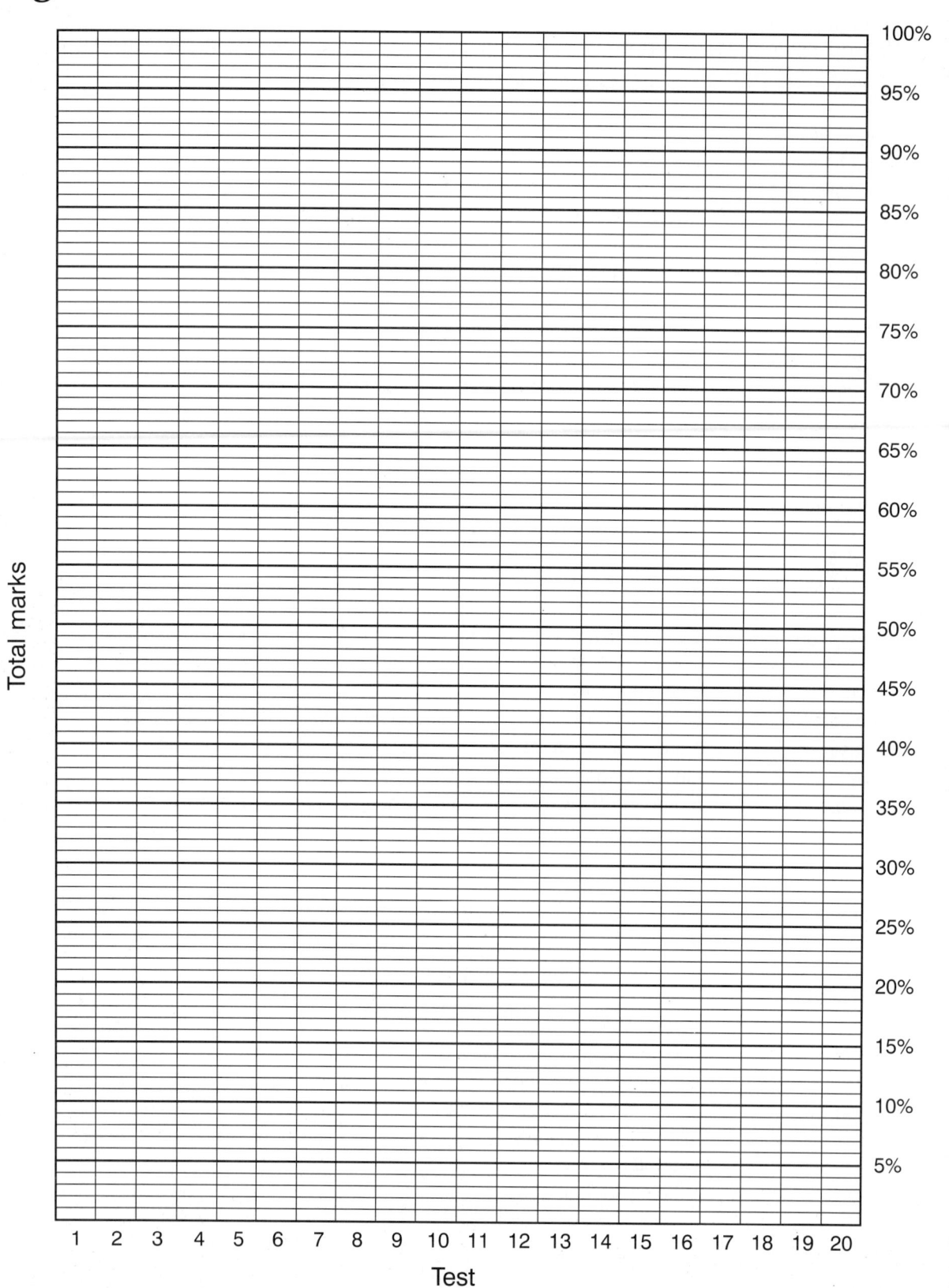

Total marks (y-axis: 5% to 100% in 5% increments)

Test (x-axis: 1 to 20)

48